SEVEN WRONG
RELATIONSHIPS

ALSO FROM REVIVAL TODAY

Dominion Over Sickness and Disease

Boldly I Come: Praying According to God's Word

Twenty Secrets for an Unbreakable Marriage

How to Dominate in a Wicked Nation

Seven Wrong Relationships

Books are available in EBOOK and PAPERBACK through your favorite online book retailer or by request from your local book store.

SEVEN WRONG
RELATIONSHIPS

JONATHAN SHUTTLESWORTH

Book design by eBook Prep:
www.ebookprep.com

April 2022
ISBN: 978-1-64457-290-0

Rise UP Publications
644 Shrewsbury Commons Ave
Ste 249
Shrewsbury PA 17361
United States of America

www.riseUPpublications.com
Phone: 866-846-5123

CONTENTS

INTRODUCTION

There are people who the Devil has sent to destroy you. You must possess a thought process that says, "I have dominion, particularly in the realm of my own life. My life will not be determined by other people; my life will be determined by the decisions I make."

You must decide to identify and dominate the people sent to destroy your life.

Jesus taught about wolves, sheep, wolves in sheep's clothing, goats, and shepherds. Not everyone is the same.

"Well, I think we should treat everybody equally."

I don't. I don't treat my wife the same as the FedEx driver. What a stupid way of thinking. You shouldn't give preferential treatment to people because they're rich. You'd be a fool to treat everybody the same.

Suppose the FedEx lady comes to my house, and I give her a huge kiss. My wife, upon seeing this, draws her gun and says, "What are you doing?"

I reply, "Well, I just feel like we should treat everybody the same. It's not right for me to be romantic with you and not with her."

You treat people differently. Whether you know it or not, you already do. You must recognize that there are people God has sent into your life to help you, and there are people the Devil has sent into your life to harm you. You have non-playable characters who have no bearing on your life, you have allies who God sends your way, and you have enemies who the Devil sends your way. The Devil can't just come and destroy your life; he uses people.

Dr. Mike Murdock said, "Whatever you don't protect, you lose." You can't be a knucklehead Christian that feels badly about throwing people out of your life who don't belong. Not everybody's looking to help you. Just as you wouldn't let snakes sleep in your bed, you don't let destructive people close to you. You have to protect yourself.

I'm going to give you seven categories of people who the Devil may send to destroy you. You will deal with these people at some point in your life. In fact, you might have all seven in your life right now. Not only are you correct in putting a wall up between you and them, but you're also wrong not to.

NUMBER ONE

THOSE WHO USURP YOUR AUTHORITY

You should take it seriously when somebody tries to usurp your authority.

Why pastors submit to a board of people who aren't in the ministry is beyond me. Do you know what I know about aeronautics? Nothing. Do you know how many aeronautics boards I sit on? None. Why would you discuss ministry things with people who've never been in the ministry a day in their lives?

I know a good pastor who is not in the ministry anymore; this was one of the things that took him out. He had a board made up of people elected out of his church's congregation, which is a mistake. It's modeled after the American government; it's not scriptural. This pastor would sit on one side of the table, and another guy who was a doctor would sit on the other side of the table. Everything the pastor felt to do, the doctor would shoot it down.

The doctor would say, "Well, I'm the chairman of the board here."

When you read the book of Revelation, God didn't say, "Write these letters to the seven chairmen of the board of the churches at Thyatira, Laodicea or Philadelphia." He said, "Write it to the angel of the church." Angel refers to the pastor.

Almost everybody on our staff graduated from River University, and RBI does a fantastic job of teaching respect for authority. I've never said something like, "Listen, let's buy a video wall for the background," and had a staff member say, "No, I don't think that's a good idea." I've never had someone on my staff challenge my authority. If anybody that works here at Revival Today, after I gave them instruction, said, "You do things your way, and I'll do things my way," it's over. No discussion. It's just over.

Jesus took it very seriously when Peter challenged his authority in public. Jesus said, "I must go to Jerusalem."

Peter said, "Stop saying you're going to go to Jerusalem."

The Bible says Jesus looked at the other disciples, like 'pay attention,' and then looked at Peter and said, "Get thee behind me, Satan."

When you're a leader, and somebody publicly challenges your authority in front of those whom you're in authority over, you should respond in such a way that it will never happen again.

I was at a meeting run by a great man of God. The minister running the meeting asked another minister to sing one song and told him which song to sing. Instead of doing what was asked of him, that man preached for 45 minutes and then sang three songs.

When he finished singing and gave the microphone back, the pastor rebuked him for about 30 minutes; it was a strong rebuke. Do you know that's scriptural?

Evangelist R.W. Schambach was praying for the sick, going down the prayer line. He gets to a lady, who, as he's about to lay hands on her, lays into brother Schambach.

"You took over an hour on the offering. People are sick here. They didn't come here for you to take an offering...."

She keeps going on and on.

Brother Schambach was a real nice guy, so he just skips her and moves down the line. Later, the Lord spoke to him and said, "Until you deal with her, no one else will be healed because she's taken your authority away in the spirit."

Deal with people who usurp your authority.

I was about 24 years old, preaching in Montreal, we were having revival meetings. As I was praying for people, an assistant pastor at the church got right up in my face—I mean mid-service—and says "Brother, you are pushing the people down." He thought I was pushing people down when they were actually falling under the power of God. I was taught to respect my elders; he was older than me—everybody in the meeting was older than me. However, I felt the Holy Ghost rise up within me. I put my finger in his face and started walking towards him while he started backing up. I said, "Sit down and shut up and stay out of my way the rest of the time I'm here. Do you understand me?"

I backed him up to the first row; he sat down and nodded his head. "Yes," I said, "say yes, sir."…and he said, "yes, sir."

We had revival that week.

Rebellion is the same as the sin of witchcraft, and rebellion is overstepping authority. Let me ask you a question: What sin did Satan commit to get thrown out of heaven? Did he have sex with another angel? Did he steal some of the gold off the street? What did he do? He tried to overstep God's authority.

Satan said, "I will ascend and be like the most high God."

What did God do in response? Hug him? Did he say something like, "Hey, I heard you're trying to be like me, and you know, that's not really right, so..."

No, you don't coddle snakes. Rebellion is just like the sin of witchcraft. God doesn't tolerate that, and neither should you. Don't let people usurp your authority, especially in the ministry.

Luke 10:18, "I saw Satan fall like lightning out of heaven."

One thing I can't relate to is people saying, "Well, wait until your kid becomes a teenager. You know, they're hard to control."

No, my child *will* listen. I can get demons to listen. I *will* get my child to obey.

Growing up, disobedience was never tolerated in my home. The last time I got paddled, I was 12 years old. It wasn't like my dad had to beat me into submission; it was authority. The times I got paddled were times when I was usurping other people's authority, not my dad's, not my mother's.

If you can't even get your dog to listen to you, you're going to have problems in the ministry. Without authority, you're going to have problems raising children.

The Devil sends people to usurp your authority in whatever position he's given you, and you can't allow it. There's a way to establish your authority and keep things in line, but you need to understand what's needed and do it.

Now, if someone is in authority over you, that's another story. But whatever realm God has put you in authority over, you treat any attempt to usurp that authority as a satanic attack.

NUMBER TWO

THOSE WHO STEAL YOUR PEACE

Has there ever been somebody in your life, like a coworker, whose presence affected your sleep? Maybe you left work at 5:00 PM, and even by 11:30 PM, you were wide awake because of the thought of them— what they were doing, what they had done, and knowing that you're going to see them tomorrow.

Troublemakers. The Bible speaks of a category of people called troublemakers.

God gives you peace. Satan attempts to steal what God gives. Not just money, not just health, but also peace. Christians think it's wrong to take a stand against somebody. However, it's wrong to *not* take a stand against troublemakers; Jesus never tried to convert the Pharisees and Sadducees.

> Alexander the coppersmith did me much
> harm, but the Lord will judge him for

what he has done. Be careful of him, for
he fought against everything we said.

— 2 TIMOTHY 4:14

Timothy, my son, here are my instructions
for you, based on the prophetic words
spoken about you earlier. May they help
you fight well in the Lord's battles.
Cling to your faith in Christ, and keep
your conscience clear. For some people
have deliberately violated their
consciences; as a result, their faith has
been shipwrecked. Hymenaeus and
Alexander are two examples. I threw
them out and handed them over to Satan
so they might learn not to blaspheme
God.

— 1 TIMOTHY 1:18-20

One of them, according to Dake, was a man who thrust
away and made a shipwreck of his faith, becoming a
blasphemer. The other was a false teacher who overthrew
the faith of others.

Avoid worthless, foolish talk that only leads
to more godless behavior. This kind of
talk spreads like cancer, as in the case of
Hymenaeus and Philetus. They have left
the path of truth, claiming that the

> resurrection of the dead has already
> occurred; in this way, they have turned
> some people away from the faith.

— 2 TIMOTHY 2:16-18

Paul said there are people who overthrew other people's faith by what they did. What was Paul's response to these people? Did Paul say, *"Let's pray for them?"* No. Paul said, *"I've turned them over to Satan that they might learn not to blaspheme God."* Is that in the Old Testament or New Testament? New Testament.

Some might respond to that and say, "Well, I thought you're supposed to be a Christian," and they would be confused on what it means to be a Christian. Not only was Paul a Christian, he was like Captain Christian, and he said he turned those who wrecked the faith of others over to Satan.

> But Elymas, the sorcerer (as his name
>   means in Greek), interfered and urged
>   the governor to pay no attention to what
>   Barnabas and Saul said. He was trying
>   to keep the governor from believing.
> Saul, also known as Paul, was filled with
>   the Holy Spirit, and he looked the
>   sorcerer in the eye. Then he said, "You
>   son of the devil, full of every sort of
>   deceit and fraud, and enemy of all that
>   is good! Will you never stop perverting

the true ways of the Lord? Watch now,
for the Lord has laid his hand of
punishment upon you, and you will be
struck blind. You will not see the
sunlight for some time." Instantly mist
and darkness came over the man's eyes,
and he began groping around begging
for someone to take his hand and
lead him.
When the governor saw what had
happened, he became a believer, for he
was astonished at the teaching about the
Lord.

— ACTS 13:8-12

Back when pastors started closing their churches, around March 12th 2020, one pastor wrote that he was closing his church because he wanted his church-goers to be good citizens and all that. I retweeted his church closure announcement and added the rolling-eye emoji above it.

On March 12th he tweets, "Here's an idea, partner with your city rather than act like the government is trying to destroy the church. Relax. Sometimes, the best evangelism is cooperation."

Fast forward to May 16th, he tweets, "I've got to admit, the way our mayor said we will never return to normal until we find a vaccine made me think of going to a different city to start another church."

Then his next tweet, "If leaders 100% intention for excessive lockdown was to save lives, we could at least understand and even go along. However, when people are being used as bargaining chips for more bailout money to build a new Los Angeles, well, that's just ransom."

What happened to relaxing? You know, many people are going to go to hell because they relaxed. David fell into sin with Bathsheba when he relaxed. The Bible says, "Be alert and on guard."

I could have told that guy on March 12th 2020, that the mayor's not your friend, that mayor used you for free food, free backpack giveaways, and photography for elections.

It's amazing how many pastors thought they had a good relationship with their city, and next thing you know, the same city said they wouldn't allow them to have church.

You realize that the relationship was one way. Those pastors can't see it. They're blind. They think everybody's their friend.

Jesus said to be wise as serpents, harmless as doves. Most Christians get an "A+" in harmless as doves and an "F" in wise as serpents.

People tend to keep those close to them who are destructive without fully realizing what they are doing, but you have to keep an eye on people because they change.

When Jesus brought Judas with him, Judas was fine. But the Bible says, *"Later on, the Devil entered into Judas."* The Devil wasn't in Judas when he started traveling.

People can change, sometimes people go nuts. You hire somebody, they're fine. They're on fire for God. Then they get a drinking problem. They start doing drugs. You don't know what's going on behind the scenes.

You have to stay in prayer, and you have to constantly evaluate the people around you. If somebody starts to not feel right anymore, something's wrong.

My grandfather, A.E. Shuttlesworth, used to say, "Problems in life are free. You don't have to put them on the payroll." Don't pay people who cause problems.

When you get to the place where you can hire people, you're to hire people to take things off your plate, not put things on your plate.

People who steal your peace are not from God.

NUMBER THREE

THOSE WHO STEAL YOUR JOY

The third of the seven people who need to exit your life are people who steal your joy; people who steal your enthusiasm.

For example, when you get a God-idea and you say, "Man, the Lord just gave me this idea. I'm going to do this, and I bet we'll have double the effectiveness by the end of the year compared to what we have right now." This type of person would respond with, "Oh, hold your breath. I guess it's going to cost a lot of money."

Then all your enthusiasm and passion is immediately sucked out by some demon-anointed person who makes it their business to steal your joy.

Why is your joy important?

> "Go and celebrate with a feast of rich foods
> and sweet drinks, and share gifts of food

> with people who have nothing prepared.
> This is a sacred day before our Lord.
> Don't be dejected and sad, for the joy of
> the LORD is your strength!"

— NEHEMIAH 8:10

The joy of the Lord is your strength. It takes strength to conquer, get to your destiny, and get to the goal God has given you in life.

You don't get there being weak; you have to be strong. So, the Devil sends people to try to sap your joy. You get off the phone with them after eight minutes, and you feel like you need an hour-long nap to recover.

Anything you don't protect, you lose. Just like you protect your holiness, you protect your marriage, and you protect your children, in the same way, you need to protect your joy. Guard it, seed your joy, increase your joy, put people around you who make you happy.

The skills people have are only half of the reason why we hire them at Revival Today. The other half is that they make me happy when they're around.

Some pastors dread going to their offices because the staff they hired are a bunch of miserable, depressed people. If you walk into most church offices on a Tuesday, you'd think it was a funeral parlor. I couldn't work with people like that; there should be enthusiasm and joy.

Hire young, energetic people and don't turn them into old people. Don't hire people who act like they died two weeks ago. You should hire people who make you look forward to coming to wherever you work.

Feed your joy.

There are little things you can do to feed your joy. For example, I have a mug from my favorite resort, The Phoenician, in Scottsdale, Arizona. When I look at that mug, memories flood back from being there with my wife, Adalis, and my daughter, Camila. One day, I think Camila and I swam from 10:00 AM to 8:00 PM; the whole time, we never got out of the water. That was one of the best days I've ever had in my life, and that mug takes a piece of that and puts it in me. You can do little things to feed your joy—you don't just protect your joy; you feed your joy.

Happiness is a good thing. I have a favorite drink, and I keep four or five in my refrigerator at work. I'm happier drinking an iced caramel coffee than I am not drinking an iced caramel coffee. So, I have things waiting where I work that make me happy.

Put things on your walls that make you happy. What's your favorite picture? Don't have a picture on your wall of somebody that died. If you lost a family member, keep their photos somewhere to look at them when you are ready. You don't need it greeting you in your living room every morning; it will be the first thing snapping you out of a good mood.

Guard your joy against those anointed by the Devil to steal it because your joy is your strength. The joy of the Lord is your strength, recognize that the Devil sends people to steal your joy.

NUMBER FOUR

THOSE WHO FEED YOUR CARNAL NATURE

Get rid of anybody in your life who feeds your carnal nature.

> Now David's son Absalom had a beautiful sister named Tamar. And Amnon, her half brother, fell desperately in love with her. Amnon became so obsessed with Tamar that he became ill. She was a virgin, and Amnon thought he could never have her.
> But Amnon had a very crafty friend—his cousin Jonadab. He was the son of David's brother Shimea. One day Jonadab said to Amnon, "What's the trouble? Why should the son of a king look so dejected morning after morning?"
> So Amnon told him, "I am in love with Tamar, my brother Absalom's sister."

"Well," Jonadab said, "I'll tell you what to do. Go back to bed and pretend you are ill. When your father comes to see you, ask him to let Tamar come and prepare some food for you. Tell him you'll feel better if she prepares it as you watch and feeds you with her own hands."

So Amnon lay down and pretended to be sick. And when the king came to see him, Amnon asked him, "Please let my sister Tamar come and cook my favorite dish as I watch. Then I can eat it from her own hands." So David agreed and sent Tamar to Amnon's house to prepare some food for him.

When Tamar arrived at Amnon's house, she went to the place where he was lying down so he could watch her mix some dough. Then she baked his favorite dish for him. But when she set the serving tray before him, he refused to eat. "Everyone get out of here," Amnon told his servants. So they all left.

Then he said to Tamar, "Now bring the food into my bedroom and feed it to me here." So Tamar took his favorite dish to him. But as she was feeding him, he grabbed her and demanded, "Come to bed with me, my darling sister."

"No, my brother!" she cried. "Don't be foolish! Don't do this to me! Such

wicked things aren't done in Israel.
Where could I go in my shame? And
you would be called one of the greatest
fools in Israel. Please, just speak to the
king about it, and he will let you
marry me."

But Amnon wouldn't listen to her, and since
he was stronger than she was, he raped
her. Then suddenly Amnon's love
turned to hate, and he hated her even
more than he had loved her. "Get out of
here!" he snarled at her.

— 2 SAMUEL 13:1-14

Amnon didn't have the guts to do that, but he had a friend named Jonadab who encouraged him to sin. Amnon liked that girl. He knew it was wrong to want that girl. Then somebody came into his life and steered him in the wrong direction, saying, "No, do it, man. In fact, I'll tell you how to do it." Some of you have people like that in your life right now. If you wanted to have an affair, they'd buy your hotel room for you. They'll let you use their car. They'd take steps to make sure your spouse doesn't find out. Get those people out of your life.

Do you know why I've never had any alcohol in my life? I've never known anybody who drank alcohol. I was never offered any; I wasn't around it. It's very easy to not sin when there's no temptation to sin.

Do you know why I've never smoked marijuana? I've never been around it. I don't know where to buy it. I don't know where you get papers to roll it. I know they exist; I don't know where you get them. I don't know how to roll it. I don't think I even own a lighter.

As a teenager, I didn't have people pressuring me to have sex. I would walk into a room, and if anyone was doing something they shouldn't have been, they'd say, "Hey, Jonathan's here, just put that away until he's gone." I must have carried myself in such a way that people would not do or say certain things around me out of respect, even in high school.

Remove people from your life who feed your carnal and sinful nature.

NUMBER FIVE

THOSE WHO MOCK YOUR FAITH

R emove people from your life who mock your faith. And by that, I don't mean mock Christianity; they mock *your* faith.

When you start living for the Lord, some people will give you a hard time for going to church. These people, anointed by the Devil, will say, "You don't have to go to church. Church is just a building. God's presence is everywhere. God is in your house. You know, I think God's not just in the sky, he's everywhere."

You don't want to spend a lot of time with people like that.

Get the people out of your life who mock you when you start to move into the deeper things of God. Paul said, "I desired to feed you meat, but you were only ready for milk."

Maybe when you started to understand healing or prosperity, you shared it with your family or your friends, expecting to get a favorable response, something like,

"Yeah, that's true. I should start giving too. God will break me out like he's breaking you out."

But instead, you got the exact opposite reaction. They said, "I'd be careful about that if I were you."

Look out for people who discourage your faith. The Devil can't stop faith from working, but he can put people in your life who speak against tithing, being faithful to church, blessing your pastor, believing in healing, and believing in the deeper things of God.

There are actually people who will try to pull you back into the shallow things of God by mocking your faith; you need to be able to recognize and remove them.

NUMBER SIX

THOSE WHO TRY TO BLOCK YOUR ADVANCEMENT

You have to remove people who outright try to block your advancement. You oppose those people. You oppose them in prayer. You oppose them with your words. You let God anoint your mind to make a plan.

> Then I told them about how the gracious
>   hand of God had been on me, and about
>   my conversation with the king.
> They replied at once, "Yes, let's rebuild the
>   wall!" So they began the good work.
> But when Sanballat, Tobiah, and Geshem
>   the Arab heard of our plan, they scoffed
>   contemptuously. "What are you doing?
>   Are you rebelling against the king?"
>   they asked.
> I replied, "The God of heaven will help us
>   succeed. We, his servants, will start
>   rebuilding this wall. But you have no

share, legal right, or historic claim in Jerusalem."

— NEHEMIAH 2:18-20

"I don't see anywhere in the Bible where God ever built a wall to keep people out."

Sorry that you bought a Bible with the book of Nehemiah ripped out. But there's a whole book in the Bible about God anointing two men, Nehemiah and Ezra, to build a wall to keep enemies out.

"Show me somewhere in the Bible where God ever shut anybody out."

Start with the fall of Adam and Eve, and them being kicked out of the garden. Then you can go to Noah with people sealed out of the boat, then you can go to Nehemiah with a literal wall being built to keep enemies out. God anointed these people to shut their enemies out, and when He anointed Nehemiah to rebuild the wall, the Devil anointed three guys, Sanballat, Tobiah, and Geshem, to oppose them. They opposed them throughout the whole book. And as soon as they opposed them, Nehemiah didn't just drop his shoulders and stay quiet. He said, "I'm going to build this wall, and you'll have no share of it. And you won't stop it."

There will be people who make it their business to see that you don't succeed. Some people are more interested in my ministry than I am. It's only a matter of time before somebody has a YouTube channel dedicated to saying why

I'm from the Devil. The Devil anoints somebody to be obsessed with you failing.

Not everybody's your friend. The Devil raises up enemies, but you know what God said? If you stick with Him, He will prepare a table for you in the presence of your enemies.

I prophesy in the name of Jesus, everyone making a plan to keep you bound and to keep you small, from today, their plans are cut down.

NUMBER SEVEN

THOSE WHO ARE A THIRD VOICE IN MARRIAGE

When Adam and Eve were in the garden, everything was fine until something ruined it. What ruined their garden? A third voice comes in the form of a serpent and introduces a new train of thought to Adam and Eve that separates them from God, bringing sin. That messes up their marriage, which results in their children being messed up. Get rid of any third voice in your marriage.

I've had people tell me, "My mother-in-law calls all the time and says stuff that bothers my wife and speaks against me. What should I do?"

I thank God I was blessed with a great mother-in-law. But I'm telling you, as a man, if somebody called my home, bothered my wife, and spoke against me, it would happen only one time.

Imagine if Eve would've yanked that serpent out of the tree, cut its head off, and served snake soup that night. We'd be living a different story right now.

Don't allow a third voice into your marriage.

I'm not talking about your pastor. I'm talking about one of your old girlfriends, the ones who call and say, "You think he treats you right? Because me and Marsha have been talking, and we don't think he treats you right."

Get rid of them. You know you don't have to answer your phone; that's not a revelation to many people. There's a thing called caller ID now, and I use it well. I don't have random conversations; my time is very valuable.

Don't allow a third voice in your marriage; what God has joined together, no one should tear apart.

Don't be a third voice in someone else's marriage, either. The Bible clearly says in Proverbs that only a fool makes up his mind about a matter without hearing both sides of the story. Don't let people drag you into their problems, and don't let people come in and create a problem for you. I know people making decisions right now, and I know it's the wrong decision, but they won't hear one word out of me. They would have if I was 24, I used to tell everybody everything. Maybe if you ask, I'll tell you. But I found that most people don't really want your advice, even if they ask. They want you to affirm what they've already decided to do. You'll waste your life thinking you're God's gift to the earth to help and sort everybody's problems out.

Make it your goal to live a quiet life,
    minding your own business and
    working with your hands, just as we
    instructed you before. Then people who
    are not believers will respect the way
    you live, and you will not need to
    depend on others.

—1 THESSALONIANS 4:11-12

AFTERWORD

Not only has God put people in your life to help you, but there are also people who the Devil has sent your way to harm you. The Devil can't come in and destroy your life when you're a born-again believer, but he can send destructive people your way. The seven types of wrong relationships are: the one that usurps your authority, the one that steals your peace, the one that steals your joy, the one that feeds your carnal nature, the one that mocks your faith, the one that blocks your advancement, and the one that is a third voice in your marriage.

If you find yourself with one or more of these relationships in your life, get rid of them. Not only is it imperative to recognize these people, you also need to remove them. Don't stand by and allow your life to be negatively dictated by the actions of those around you.

When Peter stepped out of line and tried to usurp Jesus's authority, Jesus dealt with him harshly. When Nehemiah faced opposition when building his wall, he stood strong against those who stood in the way of his advancement. Don't coddle the people who fit into these descriptions. Take authority and come to the complete realization that you have dominion over your life and that your life will not be dictated by others.

> "Look, I am sending you out as sheep
> among wolves. So be as shrewd as
> snakes and harmless as doves."

> — MATTHEW 10:16

ABOUT THE AUTHOR

Evangelist and Pastor, Jonathan Shuttlesworth, is the founder of Revival Today and Pastor of Revival Today Church, ministries dedicated to reaching lost and hurting people with The Gospel of Jesus Christ.

In fulfilling his calling, Jonathan Shuttlesworth has conducted meetings and open-air crusades throughout North America, India, the Caribbean, and Central and South Africa.

Revival Today Church was launched in 2022 as a soul-winning, Holy Spirit honoring church that is unapologetic about believing the Bible to bless families and nations.

Each day thousands of lives are impacted globally through Revival Today Broadcasting and Revival Today Church, located in Pittsburgh, Pennsylvania.

While methods may change, Revival Today's heartbeat remains for the lost, providing biblical teaching on faith, healing, prosperity, freedom from sin, and living a victorious life.

If you need help or would like to partner with Revival Today to see this generation and nation transformed through The Gospel, follow these links…

Contact Revival Today

www.RevivalToday.com
www.RevivalTodayChurch.com

facebook.com/revivaltoday
twitter.com/jdshuttlesworth
instagram.com/jdshuttlesworth
youtube.com/RevivalToday07

CPSIA information can be obtained
at www.ICGtesting.com
Printed in the USA
BVHW051950240722
642641BV00001B/3

9 781644 572900